DEGAS

Degas

by Eduard Hüttinger

CROWN TRADE PAPERBACKS · NEW YORK

Title page: SELF-PORTRAIT, 1857
Etching, II/V
The Metropolitan Museum of Art, New York

Series published under the direction of:
MADELEINE LEDIVELEC-GLOECKNER

Illustrations and layout:
MARIE-HÉLÈNE AGÜEROS

Translated from the German by:
ELLEN HEALY

Published by Crown Trade Paperbacks, 201 East 50th Street,
New York, New York 10022.
Member of the Crown Publishing Group.

Random House, Inc. New York,
Toronto, London, Sydney, Auckland

CROWN TRADE PAPERBACKS and colophon are trademarks of
Crown Publishers, Inc. Originally published in hardcover by
Crown Publishers, Inc., in 1977.

Printed in Italy - Poligrafiche Bolis S.P.A., Bergamo

Library of Congress Cataloging-in-Publication Data

Hüttinger, Eduard.
Degas.
(Crown art library)
1. Degas, Edgar, 1834 –1917—Criticism and
interpretation. 2. Impressionism (Art)—France.
3. Paris (France) in art. I. Degas, Edgar, 1834–1917.
II. Title. III. Series.
N6853.D33H88 1988 759.4 87-36394

ISBN 0-517-88418-6

10 9 8 7 6 5 4 3 2 1

First Paperback Edition

JEPHTHAH'S DAUGHTER, 1859-1860. Oil on canvas, 77″ × 117½″ (183 × 296 cm)
Smith College Museum of Art, Northampton, Massachusetts

It is difficult to define precisely and briefly the place of Edgar Degas in nineteenth-century French painting. Most of the great painters of the nineteenth century belong to one of the various trends of the period, so that the essential features of their work are clearly revealed. Jean-Dominique Ingres is identified with Classicism; Eugène Delacroix with Romanticism; Gustave Courbet with Realism; Claude Monet, Alfred Sisley, Camille Pissarro, and — albeit to a lesser degree — Edouard Manet and Auguste Renoir with Impressionism; and finally, Georges Seurat and Paul Signac with Neo-Impressionism. Degas, however, stands in a category by himself. He was inspired by the classical style of Ingres; he also showed touches of Realism, and, to a greater extent, of Impressionism. But he never belonged to any of these trends, remaining fiercely independent throughout

Baroness Bellelli, ca 1858
Pencil with green gouache on beige paper
10¼″ × 8″ (26.1 × 20.4 cm)
Cabinet des Dessins, Musée du Louvre, Paris

his life, both as a man and as an artist. Degas's paintings cover a wide span in the history of nineteenth-century art, from Classicism to Fauvism. No single school can account for his works, which are rooted in his complex personality. His artistic development followed its own compelling rules, which he discovered in the solitude of his studio, and his individualism was matched only by that of Paul Cézanne, however different these two masters may have been in other respects. Degas and Cézanne were the great loners of nineteenth-century painting, at a time when there were so many communities of artists sharing the same ideas about art.

Degas came at a crucial moment in history. As a result of the upheaval caused by the French Revolution, the traditional — but eroding — unity of art and religion had finally been destroyed. With the Revolution, art broke away from mysticism and Europe's hitherto solid social structure had crumbled. Artists were increasingly isolated. Ingres had achieved a certain status as director of the Académie de Rome. Later, when he returned to Paris, he received numerous official honors and was able to enjoy the status due to a major artist. However, Ingres was a classicist and as such he could claim to belong to a specific tradition. Unlike Ingres, Delacroix had chosen to put a very personal interpretation on the art and literature of the past, but he had done this at the price of cutting himself off from the public: The Christian and mystical themes of his works were no longer popular, and his paintings showed a touch of melancholy and pathos which made them too unusual for the times. By the 1850s, Western Europe was in intellectual and political turmoil and all major artistic work was done in isolation. Ingres's classicism fostered many followers, but they merely developed the sterile academic style of the Ecole des Beaux-Arts. And Delacroix's romanticism was not destined to create a school of lasting influence.

This was the situation when Degas started painting. He was a classicist for a short time. Later, however, he broke away from traditional patterns and created a style of his own to depict the world of the stage and the racecourse. While landscapes dominate the work of the other Impressionists, Degas never regarded himself as a landscape painter. He was not interested in nature as such, whether in the countryside or in the contrived arrangements of still lifes. With a remarkable consistency, Degas focused on man, recording the most unusual positions of the human body in drawings which were both precise and vivid. He gave pride of place to drawings over all other techniques and this is where he differed most from his contemporaries. This predilection for drawing stemmed from Degas's respect for the old masters. Degas used a classicist technique, with its emphasis on clean lines, to catch a fleeting moment of contemporary life. In one of the notebooks he wrote as a young man, Degas himself pointed to the tension that such endeavor must create, when he begged Giotto not to stand before Paris and Paris not to obscure Giotto's paintings. Thus he could define the structure of his own style: the great Western tradition of Classicism combined with the direct and passionate observation of the modern age.

Portrait of Gennaro Bellelli, 1860
Pencil, 10⅝" × 8½" (27.2 × 22.7 cm)
Cabinet des Dessins, Musée du Louvre, Paris

Degas was a lonely man, and this was due as much to his personality as to his ideas about art. In his letters he often alluded to the fact that he needed to be alone to do his work. It may be that at first he made a virtue of his distress at not being understood by those circles which traditionally provided artists with patrons. While this loneliness was caused by the circumstances under which he worked, it accounted in turn for his behavior and character as they were perceived and handed down by contemporaries. He was a sarcastic man, who could not resist delivering caustic remarks which often hurt the people around

*Study for the Portrait of Madame Hertel
(A Woman with Chrysanthemums), 1865
Pencil, 14″ × 9″ (35.7 × 23.3 cm)
Fogg Art Museum
Cambridge, Massachusetts
Bequest of Meta and Paul J. Sachs*

him.[1] He was also a sensitive man hiding under a skeptical guise, and this may have led people to accuse him of being heartless and cold; it may even have endangered his friendship with other artists. Clearly, his contemporaries, in particular Ambroise Vollard, who was prone to irony himself — drew exaggerated pictures of Degas which border on caricature. Georges Rivière was more perceptive and closer to reality when he wrote that Degas was a "false misanthropist." Everything — his cutting coldness, his cruelty and acute perception which could lay men bare — everything was really only a veneer of self-protection beneath which lay an easily wounded heart. As an artist, Degas enjoyed great esteem among a close circle of fellow artists and friends, in spite of occasional quarrels. Manet and Renoir were among his friends, as well as Monet, Armand Guillaumin, Paul Gauguin, and Vincent van Gogh. Finally, Degas strongly influenced the art of his time without ever wishing to do so — suffice it to mention the names of Manet, Mary Cassatt, Jean-Louis Forain, Gauguin, Henri de Toulouse-Lautrec, Suzanne Valadon, and Edouard Vuillard. To the end he was a faithful friend to the comrades of his youth, Paul Valpinçon and Henri and Alexis Rouart. The Dreyfus affair tore the whole of French society apart and Degas's siding with those opposed to Dreyfus brought about his separation from Monet and the writer Ludovic Halévy. The sculptor Albert Bartholomé, however, remained one of his closest friends. The position adopted by Degas over the Dreyfus affair had

(1) Wilhelm Hausenstein, *Degas*. Bern: Alfred Scherz, 1948, p. 12.

A WOMAN WITH CHRYSANTHEMUMS, 1858-1865
Oil on canvas, 29″ × 36½″ (73.7 × 92.7 cm)
The Metropolitan Museum of Art, New York
Bequest of Mrs. H.O. Havemeyer

THE BELLELLI FAMILY
ca 1860
Oil on canvas
78¾″ × 99½″ (200 × 253 cm)
Musée d'Orsay, Paris

Portrait of Giulia Bellelli, 1858-1859
Black pencil, gray wash, turpentine
and white highlights on off-white paper
9¹/₁₆″ × 7⅞″ (23.4 × 19.6 cm)
Cabinet des Dessins, Musée du Louvre, Paris

Portrait of Giovanna Bellelli, 1858-1859
Black pencil and stump on pink paper
13″ × 9⁷/₁₆″ (32.6 × 23.8 cm)
Cabinet des Dessins, Musée du Louvre, Paris

◁

PORTRAIT OF THÉRÈSE DE GAS, ca 1863
Oil on canvas, 35″ × 26⅜″ (89 × 67 cm)
Musée d'Orsay, Paris

13

PORTRAIT OF HORTENSE VALPINÇON AS A CHILD, 1871
Oil on canvas, 29⅜″ × 44¾″ (75.5 × 113.8 cm)
The Minneapolis Institute of Art, Minnesota
The John R. Van Derlip Fund

14

DOUBLE PORTRAIT - THE COUSINS OF THE PAINTER, ca 1865
Oil on canvas, 22⁷⁄₁₆″ × 27⁹⁄₁₆″ (57 × 70 cm)
The Wadswoth Atheneum, Hartford, Connecticut
The Ella Gallup Sumner and Mary Catlin Sumner Collection

its roots in aristocratic conservatism, loathing of mass movements and democracy, and an antisemitism traditional among members of his class.

Degas was consistent in his opinion that artists should not have any romantic involvement beside their art. He never married and nobody knew him to have had love affairs. It could be said that his private life was not successful, but what may appear as a lack of emotional fulfillment was the prerequisite for the freedom of his art, the price he had to pay. He valued art above all and he abided throughout his life to the principle that an artist,

> [Has] to have a high conception, not of what [he] is doing, *but of what [he] may do one day*: without that, there's no point in working. [1]

Edgar Hilaire Germain de Gas was born on July 19, 1834, at 8 Rue Saint-Georges in Paris, into a wealthy upper-middle-class Parisian family. The household seemed conventionally French and bourgeois, but it had horizons beyond Paris itself. Degas's grandmother was Italian. His grandfather, Hilaire René de Gas, had escaped from France during the French Revolution and had established himself as a prosperous banker in Naples, where he married a local girl. His father, Auguste de Gas, had come to Paris as a young man and had set up a branch of the bank. There he married Célestine Musson. Her father was a Creole born in Haiti, who had emigrated to New Orleans but had maintained connections with France, where his childen were educated. [2] It may come as a surprise that this quintessentially Parisian artist — only Manet was as much of a Parisian as he was — should not have been of entirely French descent. But this foreign element in his lineage — the de Gas family were related to the Italian aristocracy, among them Baroness Bellelli and Duchess Morbilli — may account for this uncanny ability to observe and distill the essence of Parisian life with such detachment.

Degas spent his youth in wealthy and cultured surroundings. His father loved the arts, and music above all. As the eldest son, Degas was to have taken over the banking business and was therefore intended to study law. However, he

(1) Paul Valéry, *Degas - Manet - Morisot*. Tr. by David Paul. New York: Pantheon, 1960, p. 64.
(2) Until 1865 Degas signed his name with the aristocratic spelling "de Gas". Later he simplified it to "Degas".

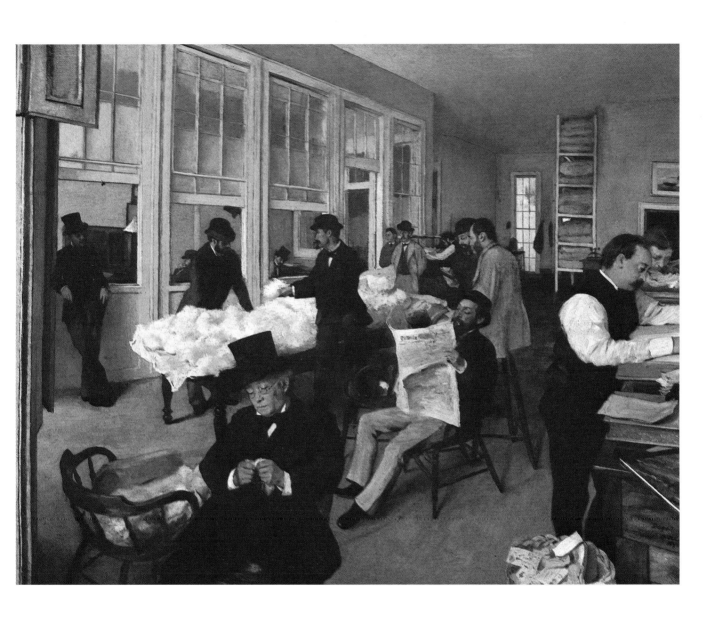

THE COTTON EXCHANGE IN NEW ORLEANS, 1873
Oil on canvas, 28¾″ × 36¼″ (74 × 92 cm)
Musée des Beaux-Arts, Pau, France

JACQUES JOSEPH (JAMES) TISSOT, 1866-1868.   Oil on canvas, 59⅝″ × 44″ (151.4 × 121.1 cm)
The Metropolitan Museum of Art, New York. The Rogers Fund

PORTRAIT OF MADAME CAMUS AT THE PIANO, 1869. Oil on canvas, 56″ × 37½″ (142.2 × 95.2 cm)
Foundation Emil G. Bührle, Zurich

proved to be a bad student. Only in drawing did he have good marks, and even as a schoolboy he had dreamed of becoming an artist. His father first put up considerable resistance, but he finally yielded to Degas's wish to study art. Unlike many nineteenth-century artists, Degas was able to devote himself to painting without a major break with his middle-class family. In 1854, at twenty years of age, he graduated from the Lycée Louis-le-Grand and briefly attended lawschool. He then enrolled in the studio of Louis Lamothe, a lackluster follower of Ingres, who favored a bloodless academic style in the tradition of Jacques-Louis David, without ever achieving David's revolutionary fervor. Degas did not learn much from Lamothe, nor from his short stay at the Ecole des Beaux-Arts in 1855. He got some technical groundings, but, more significantly, he also developed a deep admiration for Ingres, which was to last throughout his life. He viewed Lamothe as a medium through which he could have a glimpse of the art of the master. Later, an art collector and friend of his father, Edouard Valpinçon, introduced him to Ingres. On their first meeting, Ingres gave him the advice which Degas was to quote later: "Study lines, draw lots of lines, either from memory or from nature."[1] This advice remained as a precious legacy.

Degas's apprenticeship to Lamothe and work at the Ecole des Beaux-Arts might have interfered with, or even destroyed, his creative imagination. He avoided the school's stultifying influence by visiting the Louvre as often as possible, studying and copying the old masters, and particularly fifteenth-century Italian painters. In 1856 he traveled for the first time to Italy, where he intended to make the acquaintance of his Italian relatives. This journey, which was followed by another in 1858 and several more in 1859, was Degas's real education. He had long, productive stays in Naples, Rome, Florence, and Umbria. The study of the old masters, which had already begun at the Louvre and at the Cabinet des Estampes in Paris, now found its logical continuation. However, in spite of what might have been expected of a student of Lamothe and the Ecole des Beaux-Arts, it was not Raphael and the masters of the Renaissance who made the strongest impression on Degas. He preferred such fifteenth-century painters as Paolo Ucello, Benozzo Gozzoli, Ghirlandajo, Andrea Mantegna, Luca Signorelli, Perugino, and Lorenzo di Credi, or such exponents of Florentine Mannerism as Jacopo da Pontormo and Bronzino. Degas probably made drawings after

(1) Paul Valéry, *op. cit*, p. 35.

20

GIRL WITH A HAT, ca 1887-1890.   Oil on canvas, 18⅛″ × 12¾″ (46 × 32.5 cm)
Private collection. Courtesy Galerie Schmit, Paris

Michelangelo, Leonardo da Vinci, and Raphael, whether at the Louvre or in Italy, but the classical emphasis on idealism remained foreign to him. The example of David's followers had impressed on him that imitative classical form leads to empty virtuosity. By contrast, fifteenth-century Italian painting seemed to give the purest depiction of reality, of artistic truth as he saw it. He could have made this remark by Ingres, when he compared the pale imitations of David's followers with the works of Raphael: "How they misled me!" The same remark applied as Degas was discovering his selective affinity for Italian art. His attraction to Italian Primitives — as they were called from the beginning of the nineteenth century in France and Germany right into the twentieth century — was not unique at the time. At the turn of the century in France, a group around Maurice Quai, a pupil of David, had already formed an independent movement which advocated a return to the "Primitives" as a reaction against the stiff style of dying Neo-Classicism. However, their idea of primitive art was a vague notion of art before the Greek Phidias. This anti-classical and deeply literary trend soon found echos elsewhere in Europe, both among the German Lukasbrüder or Nazareners, who joined forces around 1810, and among French painters around 1830. The movement reached its zenith in 1848 with the English Pre-Raphaelite brotherhood, which was completely opposed to the "feeling of the Renaissance schools of painting, made of idleness, infidelity, sensuality, and frivolous pride." They raved

Portrait of Edouard Manet, ca 1862-1865
Etching on white wove paper II/IV
5¼" × 4¹⁵/₁₆" (13.3 × 12.5 cm)
The Philadelphia Museum of Art
Joseph E. Temple and Edgar Viguers Seelers Funds

Portrait of Diego Martelli, 1879
Black crayon and white
chalk on gray blue paper, squared up
17¾" × 11⁵/₁₆" (45 × 28.7 cm)
The Fogg Art Museum, Harvard University
Cambridge, Massachusetts

23

STUDY FOR PORTRAITS IN A FRIEZE, 1879
Oil, distemper, and pastel
19¹¹⁄₁₆″ × 25⅝″ (50 × 65 cm)
Private collection. Courtesy Galerie Schmit, Paris

about the art of the "Primitives", in which they found an almost mystical inspiration which was to help them escape from modern vulgarity. Nineteenth-century Pre-Raphaelism, be it the German, French, or English form, held no fascination for Degas. His paintings do not belong to the chain of development that led from Ingres to Pierre Puvis de Chavannes and Maurice Denis. His interpretation of fifteenth-century Italian painting transcends the context of history. His early work bears witness to the fact that he was able to absorb long past forms of art, thus following fundamental trends of his time, and give these forms a radically original content. At the beginning of his career he made copies and studies of the old masters he discovered at the Louvre and in Italy. At the same time he painted types, especially Italian women of the working classes, art studies bordering on genre painting such as the Swiss Leopold Robert and the German Nazareners had successfully cultivated. But this was only a short phase in Degas's work. His art achieved an authentic ring for the first time in the field of portrait painting, where the lessons drawn from the old masters combined with an individual mastery.

The people Degas depicted at that time were almost all members of his family, especially his sisters and brothers, and, above all, himself. There are about twenty self-portraits of that period. Later Degas did not feel the need to explore his own personality in this manner and he preferred to experiment with more objective themes. The *Self-Portrait* dated 1854-1855 is among the most complete and representative in the series.[1] It shows most strikingly how the twenty-year-old Degas wished to be seen and how he regarded himself at that time. The artist stands in front of a neutral background, arm bent, leaning against a balustrade, in a classical pose

(1) Musée d'Orsay, Paris.

Mary Cassatt at the Louvre
Museum of Antiquities, ca 1879-1880
Etching, aquatint, and drypoint, V/IX
10½″ × 9³⁄₁₆″ (26.7 × 23.5 cm)
The Toledo Museum of Art, Toledo, Ohio
Gift of Shoemaker Fund

At the Races, ca 1862
Pencil on
reddish-beige paper
13¼″ × 19″
(33.7 × 48.3 cm)
The Sterling and Francine
Clark Institute
Williamstown
Massachusetts

Four Jockeys Before the Start
of the Race, 1866-1868
Pencil on Light brown paper
15⅞″ × 15/″ (40.3 × 38.1 cm)
Collection of Mr. and
Mrs. Eugene V. Thaw, New York

which has been used over and over again since Albrecht Dürer's *Self-Portrait* [1] and Raphael's *Portrait of Angelo Doni.* [2]   This traditional style of portrait required that the model be shown not in a spontaneous or idle position, but rather in an attitude of elegant aloofness.   This Degas achieved to an unsurpassed degree in this self-portrait.   The artist we see is not a member of the carefree, daring world of bohemia, but a distinguished and serious-minded burgher.   The high, narrow shape of the canvas causes the top of his head almost to touch the upper edge of the picture.   The face has a distant, inscrutable expression, the eyes have an absent look, seemingly focused on some invisible point.   It is that same feeling and expression which, like a delicate halo, enhances portraits painted by the Mannerists, from Pontormo to Bronzino.

Degas's early portraits achieve their culmination in a work which crowns nineteenth-century portrait painting, *The Bellelli Family* (see pages 10-11).   This depicts Laura de Gas, Degas's aunt, her husband, Baron Bellelli, who was an Italian senator and a friend of Cavour, and their children Jeanne and Julie.   Degas worked

(1)   1498, Prado Museum, Madrid.
(2)   1506, Palazzo Pitti, Florence.

Study for Steeple-Chase
The Fallen Jockey, 1866
Pencil, 12⅜" × 17⅞"
(31.5 × 44.6 cm)
The Sterling and Francine
Clark Institute
Williamstown, Massachusetts

on this painting for years.   The first sketches were done in 1856 in Naples, and others, from 1857 to 1860, in Florence, where the Bellelli lived.   The painting itself was probably begun in 1857, but not finished before 1862 in Paris.   Degas was thinking of exhibiting it at the Salon, but this never happened.   The picture remained in his studio until his death, and, had it been shown at the Salon, it would undoubtedly have caused a scandal, which Degas wished to avoid for the sake of the illustrious Bellelli family.   Today, it seems inconceivable that this fear of controversy could apply to a work which has come to be regarded as the epitome of classical portrait painting.   But at the time, *The Bellelli Family* seemed revolutionary when compared with portraits accepted at the Salon, in which the subjects were required to strike a dignified and conventional pose similar to that of official, contrived photographs.   Degas's subjects do not pose as if in front of a camera; only Jeanne, one of the daughters, stares at an imaginary point in front of her.   The others are shown simply as they are.   The Baroness looks proud and erect, with a severe demeanor.   Her black dress — in 1862 she was in mourning for the death of her young son Jean — emphasizes the impression of aristocratic reserve.   Little Julie is captured in a moment of restlessness; she sits on the edge of a chair and her left leg is folded under her, out of the viewer's sight — a liberty meant to express a spontaneous directness which must have been anathema to contemporary academic painters.   There is even less of a hint of official pose in the figure of the Baron.   He is seen half from behind, sitting in a comfortable armchair and resting on his left arm, his head slightly turned toward his family, in an attitude as typical of a homelike atmosphere as the newspaper lying casually on the table next to him.   He is depicted in the intimate world of his family and this is the first indication of Degas's manner of capturing the essence of the subjects of his portraits.   This was a major departure from the canon of academic portraiture.   *The Bellelli Family* had a ring of authenticity, of directness, which set the painting apart

Horse at Trough, 1865-1881
Red Wax, h. 6⅜" (h. 16.3 cm)
Collection: Mr. and Mrs. Paul Mellon
Upperville, Virginia

Mademoiselle Fiocre in the Ballet "La Source," ca. 1866
Oil on canvas, 51³⁄₁₆″ × 57⅛″ (130 × 145)
The Brooklyn Museum, New York
Gift of J. H. Post, J. T. Underwood, and A. A. Healy

The Orchestra of the Opera, 1868-1869.   Oil on cavas, 22¼″ × 18⅛″ (56.5 × 46 cm)
Musée d'Orsay, Paris

MUSICIANS OF THE ORCHESTRA, 1872. Oil on canvas, 27⅛″ × 19¼″ (69 × 49 cm)
Städelsches Kunstinstitut, Frankfurt

THE DANCE LESSON, 1872
Oil on canvas
12½″ × 18″ (32 × 46 cm)
Musée d'Orsay, Paris

THE DANCING CLASS, ca 1871
Oil on wood, 7¾″ × 10⅝″ (19.7 × 27 cm)
The Metropolitan Museum of Art, New York
Bequest of Mrs. H.O. Havemeyer

from such other innovative portraits of the time as Ingres's drawings of family groups.

The composition, however, followed strict formal rules that are almost architectural. The crisp outline of the figures — especially that of the woman and the children — against the flat expanse of the wall, and the light giving these figures a particular density, evoke such works by Florentine Mannerists as Bronzino's portraits of the Medici. The black, gray, and white clothes combined with very clean lines add to the strong composition. Only the colors of the surroundings — the delicate blue of the wallpaper, the muted yellow of the patterned carpet, the gilt frames — make for a soft and peaceful atmosphere, while the reflection in the mirror above the fireplace creates an illusory and beguiling feeling of space.

The Bellelli Family was Degas's first original work. As a group portrait, it holds a unique place in nineteenth-century painting. Group portraits featuring representatives of a guild or managers of a company were a genre that reached its peak in the Baroque era, especially in Holland, but they had become rare in the nineteenth century. There were a few group portraits done at the time, but they usually were groups of artists who shared the same ideas about art, such as Henri Fantin-Latour's *Homage to Delacroix*,[1] *The Studio at Batignolles*,[2] and *A Corner of a Table*,[3] all of which presented their subjects in a conventional pose, very much like an official photograph. As a general rule, no social unit was sufficiently rooted in nineteenth-century reality to be deemed worthy of being represented in portraits, except for the family unit.[4] Those painters of the first half of the nineteenth century who still produced family portraits — Ingres in France, Philipp Otto Runge in Germany, Friedrich von Amerling and Heinrich Waldmüller in Austria — renounced the excessively sentimental approach of eighteenth-century portraiture, which focused on well-assorted families, happy couples, genteel home lives, and sunny children, so much so that one could rightly call these works "devotion paintings." In the nineteenth century, portraits first had to depict bourgeois dignity, often verging on ancient rigidity, and a need

(1) 1864, Musée d'Orsay, Paris.
(2) A tribute to Manet, 1870, Musée d'Orsay, Paris.
(3) Showing several men of letters grouped around Paul Verlaine and Arthur Rimbaud, 1871, Musée d'Orsay, Paris.
(4) Hermann Beeken, *Das 19. Jahrhundert in der deutschen Kunst.* Munich, 1944, p. 388.

Study for The Dancing School, 1879
Black pencil, Notebook 30, p. 17
8⅜″ × 6⅝″ (21.3 × 17 cm)
Bibliothèque nationale, Paris

to keep up appearances combined with moral austerity. With time, these criteria faded, to be replaced by a comfortable and loose arrangement of the group, which challenged the notion of a rigid and closed family. The latter type of portrait found its clearer expression in Ferdinand von Rayskis's portraits of the *Chamberlain von Schroeder and His Family*, on the steps outside Biederstein Castle, and in Degas's *Place de la Concorde*.[1] While keeping the theme of the family portrait — the Viscount Lepic with his daughters — Degas makes the public square the real subject of his painting, and the figures become passers-by, caught by chance in the frame of the picture. Therefore, *The Bellelli Family* was a cornerstone in Degas work as well as in nineteenth-century painting in general. Far removed as it is from Biedermeier prettiness and from the photographic pose, the painting once more represents the concept of the family as an institution depending on dignity, morality, and responsibility; it also shows traces of a cool detachment which was to triumph in *The Place de la Concorde*. Aside from its technical mastery, the painting draws its significance and greatness from this feeling of contrast between the self-assured family and the detached observer.

Degas's early work was also centered on historical paintings with themes drawn from religious tradition or mythology. This should not come as a surprise because, until the 1850s, the classicist doctrine regarded historical painting as the most dignified and the highest form of art, which was to hold the place occupied hitherto by religious painting, before the upheaval of the French Revolution. Suffice it to recall here the remark made by Friedrich Theodor Vischer about "History ...

(1) 1874-1875. The painting is presumed to have been destroyed.

a field for the modern artist." [1]   A young painter in Paris around 1860 who wished to exhibit at the Salon could not help turning to historical painting. Between 1860 and 1865, Degas painted five historical paintings, for which there are several sketches and versions: *Young Spartans Exercising,* [2] *Semiramis Founding a City,* [3] *Alexander and Bucephalus,* [4] *The Daughter of Jephthah* (see page 5), and *The Misfortunes of the City of Orléans,* [5] which was his first entry at the Salon.

Critics never did justice to these paintings, which is a pity, because they are very original and unlike any other historical painting in the nineteenth century.   Degas drew from many literary souces — Plutarch in the case of *Alexander and Bucephalus* and *Young Spartans* — but both the concept and the style were clear and consistent. Groups of figures appear before a wide open landscape; the figures have the three-dimensional quality of a bas-relief, and there is the same strange lack of connection between the groups and the landscape as in Florentine painting of the fifteenth century.   The figures are hardly related to each other and to their surroundings, and the groups seem to be formed in an arbitrary manner. Academicism and rationalism had stunted the creative force of myth, which, until the middle of the eighteenth century — up to the time of Giambattista Tiepolo and the painters of the later German Baroque era — inspired religious and mythological compositions with some genuine, exuberant life.   It is therefore all the more surprising that Degas succeeded in depicting the figures each in their particular individuality, with startingly intense vitality.   He transferred his

Mr. Gouffé Playing the Double Bass, ca 1869
Graphite, 7⁵⁄₁₆″ × ⅓″ 4 (18.8 × 12 cm)
Collection Mr. and Mrs. Eugene V. Thaw
New York

(1) Friedrich Theodor Vischer, *Kritische Gänge*, 1844.
(2) 1860, National Gallery, London.
(3) 1861, Musée d'Orsay, Paris.
(4) 1861-1862.
(5) 1865, Musée d'Orsay, Paris.

figures directly from his sketchbooks onto the canvas, thus preserving the movement he had captured in his sketches. Degas's historical paintings conformed entirely to the rules of classicist composition, but they were also innovative because of the freshness of his figures and the wonderfully warm colors of his landscapes. He needed only to replace his compositions after Antiquity by contemporary scenes in order to come into his own.

There were some differences in quality between Degas's historical paintings. The final version of *The Daughter of Jephthah* is probably the most successful of these early pictures.[1] It is a large canvas, 77″ × 177 1/2″, the largest one he ever painted, which seems to indicate that he regarded it as the sum of all his endeavors in the field of historical painting.[2] He had chosen a scene from the Old Testament: The Gileadite Jephthah, in return for victory against the Ammonites, promises the Lord that he will offer as a sacrifice to the Lord the first person who leaves his house to greet him on his return. Fate ordained that it should be his own daughter.[3] The painting betrays many influences, the Sienese Girolamo Genga, Cesare Sestas's *Adoration of the Magi*, and Nicolas Poussin's *The Rape of the Sabine Women*. The group of young girls evokes Sandro Botticelli. The figure of the soldier on the right, seen from the back, is reminiscent of Mantegna. Jephthah on a horse reminds one of Delacroix. The composition is

The Violonist, ca 1879
Charcoal with white highlights on blue-gray paper
16½″ × 11¾″ (42 × 30 cm)
The Museum of Fine Arts, Boston
William Francis Warden Fund

(1) The theme may have been inspired by the Abbé Barthélémy's book, *Voyage du jeune Anacharsis en Grèce*. The Italian painter Giovanni Demin had painted a fresco in 1856 on the same theme in Villa Patti, near Sedico, and Delacroix had made a sketch for a fresco intended for the Palais Bourbon in Paris, which in the end was not used. Degas must have been acquainted with both works.
(2) See Eleanor Mitchell's analysis, "La Fille de Jephté par Degas, genèse, évolution", in *Gazette des Beaux-Arts*, 1937, II, pp. 175-189.
(3) Book of Judges, Chapter 2, Verse 20.

CABARET, ca 1875-1877
Pastel over monotype
8½″ × 16″ (23.5 × 43 cm)
Corcoran Gallery of Art, Washington, D.C.
William A. Clark Collection

Music Hall Singer, 1878-1879
Black chalk with white highlights on gray paper
18¾″ × 12³⁄₁₆″ (47.5 × 31 cm)
Cabinet des Dessins, Musée du Louvre, Paris

complex, however: movement pulses through the whole canvas, and drama gives power to the work. Paul Valéry once wrote that Degas wavered between the commandments of Ingres and the strange magic of Delacroix. If Degas occasionally felt an affinity for Delacroix, it was in his *Daughter of Jephthah* that he came nearest of all to Delacroix's romanticism. In one of his studies, he made color notes, which demonstrate with what care he also developed his color scheme. Color was never for Degas a question of instinct or intuition, especially not in his early work.

> Sky gray and blue, of such intensity that the light areas stand out and the shadows seem naturally black. For the red of Jephtah's robe, remember the reddish-orange shades used for this old man in Delacroix's ... The hill with dull blue-green tones. Limit the landscape to some patches of color. Some heads raised, highlighted in profile, behind Jephthah. Grayish mush with off-white, striped belt and blue veil, slate blue with pinkish tints.[1]

The romantic undercurrent in *The Daughter of Jephthah* reappears, is even more accentuated, in the *Portrait of Mademoiselle Fiocre in the Ballet "La Source"*, painted shortly afterwards (see page 29). The theme comes from the world of the theater. Eugénie Fiocre was a ballerina at the Paris Opera, and one of her main parts was the role of Nouredda in Saint-Léon's ballet "La Source". Degas's first painting of a dancer has the charming exoticism of orientalist paintings by Théodore Chassériau or Delacroix. The theatrical setting is not taken from the reality of the stage, as in Degas's later paintings of dancers,[2] but appears as an element of romanticism, an oriental fantasy. And yet, one must not overlook such realistic details as the drinking horse. This is no longer the romantic battle horse of the Jephthah picture, but a real live study. It was no coincidence that Degas later made a clay sculpture from this horse. This touch of realism in an otherwise romantic work marks a significant step in Degas's style, when he turned away from historical painting and devoted himself to depicting contemporary scenes. Around the mid-1860s Degas had freed himself from theoretical constraints and he started to paint according to his true artistic temperament.

---

(1) Edgar Degas, "Notes pour La Fille de Jephté", in *Carnets de notes, 1868-1883*, No. 15, p. 6, Bibliothèque Nationale, Paris.
(2) "We know, however, that the elaborate decor for the Parisian production consisted of unusually veristic landscape features, including a running waterfall and a pool, and that the costumes for the piece were scrupulously oriental in design". George T.M. Shackelford. *Degas. The Dancers.* Catalogue to the exhibition at the National Gallery of Art, Washington, D.C., 1984, p. 21.

MUSIC HALL SINGER (LA CHANSON DU CHIEN), ca 1875-1877.   Gouache, pastel, and monotype on joined paper, 22⅝″ × 17⅞″ (57.5 × 45.5 cm).   Private collection. Courtesy Acquavella Galleries, New York

AUX AMBASSADEURS : MADEMOISELLE BÉCAT, 1877-1885.   Pastel over lithograph, 9¹⁄₁₆″ × 7⅞″ (23 × 20 cm)
Collection of Mr. and Mrs. Eugene V. Thaw, New York

40

There were a few external reasons for this change. Pride of place should be given to Manet's role. It was he whose *Pinic* and *Olympia*[1] laid the foundations for a new aesthetic movement, who introduced Degas to Monet, Pissarro, Renoir, Frédéric Bazille, and Cézanne. These artists would meet at the Café Guerbois in the Grande Rue des Batignolles (now Avenue de Clichy), and the circle grew to include the engravers Félix Bracquemond and Marcellin Desboutin, the painters Fantin-Latour, Guillemet, and Alfred Stevens, the draftsman Constantin Guys, and the writers Zacharie Astruc, Edmond Duranty, Philippe Burty, Emile Zola, and Théodore Duret. As early as 1845, at the end of his review of the Salon, Baudelaire spoke of the heroism of modern life and predicted that,

> The true painter …will be he who can snatch its epic quality from the life of today, and can make us see and understand, with brush or with pencil, how great and poetic we are in our cravats and our patent-leather boots.[2]

A year later, he wrote in his review of the 1846 Salon that,

> Life [in Paris] is rich in poetic and marvellous subjects. We are enveloped and steeped as though in an atmosphere of the marvellous; but we do not notice it.[3]

It was only now, at the Café Guerbois, that Baudelaire's observations and theories could find an echo. The landscapes of Camille Corot, Théodore Rousseau, François-Louis Français, Antoine Chintreuil, François Daubigny, and Henri Harpignies had given only secondary importance to the depiction of contemporary reality. Now this became the central idea of a new concept of art.

It was Duranty who influenced Degas most in this direction. The son of the writer Prosper Mérimée, Duranty was a perceptive and intelligent novelist and critic. Although Duranty's paper, "Le Réalisme," published in 1856, soon folded, his ideas revolving around contemporary life and its reflection in the arts continued to exert a widespread influence. "How can it be that we are less interesting than

(1) Musée d'Orsay, Paris.
(2) Charles Baudelaire, *Art in Paris 1845-1862*. Ed. and tr. by J. Mayne. London: Phaidon, 1965, p. 32.
(3) Charles Baudelaire, *ibid.*, p. 119.

WOMEN AT THE TERRACE OF A CAFÉ
ca 1877
Pastel, 21½″ × 28⅛″ (54.5 × 71.5 cm)
Musée d'Orsay, Paris

THE ABSINTH DRINKERS (PORTRAIT OF ELLEN ANDRÉE
AND MARCELLIN DESBOUTIN), 1876
Oil on canvas, 36¼″ × 26¾″ (92 × 68 cm)
Musée d'Orsay, Paris

our predecessors? Why have painters not followed literature, or have they adopted romantic extravagances?" were the questions Duranty kept asking. Later on, especially after 1865, Degas was to be in full accord with Duranty's ideas. And in 1876, when he summed up the discussions held at the Café Guerbois in his manifesto, "La Nouvelle Peinture", Duranty chose mostly the paintings of Degas to illustrate his point. He recommended that artists stop painting stylized figures, which he felt to be as static as vases. Instead one should look for typical traits, modern man in his daily clothes, his social surroundings, at home or in the street. This man should be observed in his privacy, with the particular traits imparted by his trade or profession. A back should reveal a man's temperament, his age, his social status; a pair of hands, a magistrate or a shopkeeper. The artist should depict men as they are in real life, with many chance gestures and subtle details of physiognomy. [1]

Apart from Duranty, the brothers Edmond and Jules de Goncourt were the only writers to have a similarly strong influence on Degas, especially with their novel "Nanette Salomon," published in 1866. The main character in the novel is an artist living in the mid-nineteenth century. Like Duranty, the Goncourts claimed that an artist should be allowed to depict modern life and choose from the motifs and themes which a large city such as Paris can offer. In 1874, Edmond de Goncourt visited Degas in his studio, and he could observe with satisfaction how much Degas's paintings were in accord with his own concept of modernity in art: "He is the man up to now who has best captured, in reproducing modern life, the soul of this life." [2]

Under the influence of these ideas, Degas's art underwent a complete change between the years 1865 and 1870. This change was the least evident in his portraits. He produced many portraits between 1863 and 1871, the major ones of which were *Thérèse de Gas (Duchess of Morbilli)* (see page 12), *Double Portrait - The Cousins of the Painter* (see page 15), *The Collector of Prints* of 1866, [3] *Madame Gaujelin* of 1867, *A Women with Chrysanthemums (Madame Hertel)* (see page 9), *Duke and Duchess of Morbilli* of 1867, [4] *Jacques Joseph (James) Tissot*

(1) Edmond Duranty, *La Nouvelle Peinture*. Paris, 1876, p. 24.
(2) Edmond de Goncourt, Feb. 13, 1874, in *Journal des Goncourts*, Volume V (1871-1877). Paris 1891, p. 112. Quoted in John Rewald, *The History of Impressionism*, 4th ed. New York: Museum of Modern Art, 1973, p. 279.
(3) The Metropolitan Museum of Art, New York.
(4) Museum of Fine Arts, Boston.

INTERIOR (THE RAPE), 1868-1869
Oil on canvas, 32″ × 45″ (81.3 × 113.5 cm)
The Philadelphia Museum of Art
The Henry P. McIlhenny Collection

THE IRONERS, ca 1884
Oil on canvas, 32⅜″ × 29¾″ (82.2 × 75.6 cm)
Norton Simon Art Foundation, Pasadena, California

46

MADEMOISELLE LALA
AT THE CIRQUE FERNANDO, 1879
Oil on canvas, 46″ × 31½″ (117 × 77 cm)
The National Gallery, London

◁

Mademoiselle Lala
at the Cirque Fernando, 1879
Black chalk and pastel on yellowish paper
18½″ × 12½″ (47 × 32 cm)
The Barber Institute of Fine Arts
Birmingham University, Great Britain

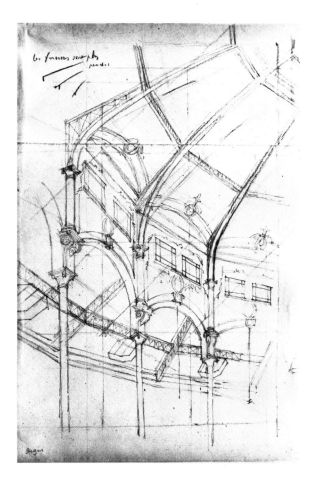

△

The Cirque Fernando
(Architectural Study), 1879
Black and red chalk on pink paper
19″ × 12½″ (48 × 31.3 cm)
The Barber Institute of Fine Arts
Birmingham University, Great Britain

Two Seated Women, ca 1878
Pastel on gray paper, 12¼″ × 18½″ (31.2 × 47 cm)
The Museum of Art, Rhode Island School of Design, Providence

(see page 18), *Mademoiselle Dihau at the Piano* of 1868,[1] *Portrait of Madame Camus at the Piano* (see page 19), *Portrait Mademoiselle Dobigny* of 1869,[2] and *Portrait of Hortense Valpinçon as a Child* (see page 14). Conventional as they may be, these portraits highlight both what is characteristic and what is casual in the personality and deportment of the sitter. Their roots go back to the heritage of such perceptive portraitists as Corneille de Lyons, François Clouet, Hans Holbein the Younger, and the major Florentine Mannerists. But Degas gave them new features, following his own motto:

> To explore the expressive possibilities of portraiture, turn an academic medium into a study of modernity... Beauty should be in any face... To make portraits of people in familiar and typical attitudes and especially give the same choice of expressions to the face that one gives to the body. For instance, if a person is a laughing type, make this person laugh.[3]

Although people are caught most of the time in a casual pose expressing the charm of a fleeting mood, formal behavior breaks through sometimes, as in the *Portrait of Madame Camus at the Piano*. She was the wife of Doctor Camus, a friend of Manet and Degas and a lover of Japanese art, and she had an excellent reputation as a pianist. The portrait still shows the faint influence of Ingres's style, but it also evokes Manet in its refined elegance. In a masterful arrangement, the

(1) Musée d'Orsay, Paris.
(2) Kunsthalle, Hamburg.
(3) Edgar Degas, *Carnets de notes, 1868-1883*. Bibliothèque Nationale, Paris. Quoted in Paul-André Lemoisne, *op. cit.*, pp. 54 and 55.

model sits in a room surrounded by angular shapes. The picture strikes a balance between a personal and an official portrait. Each detail of clothing and the surroundings — down to the incredibly delicate china figure, which throws a light shadow against the wall, and the precious, colorful frame of the mirror — is designed to draw attention to the woman: It emphasizes her culture and gracious elegance, revealing and explaining at the same time the smiling serenity in her face. Her surroundings express a harmony between the model and her art, reflecting a complex personality within the world this woman has created.

Since the art of the portrait remains more traditional, it was through the choice of new themes that Degas could best explore his ideas about a new art. He created a whole series of paintings on contemporary life, drawing themes and models from the world of the racecourse and the stage, and depicting women from the working class, milliners and women ironing.

Horse racing, a sport of English origin, became popular on the Continent at the end of the eighteenth century, and it soon inspired such painters as Charles Vernet and Théodore Géricault, who were both influenced by English artists. It also played an important part in nineteenth-century fiction, from Honoré de Balzac to Leo Tolstoy, and it was bound to attract the interest of modernist painters. Manet emphasized the elegance of these occasions, while Degas preferred to observe the horses in motion. As the other Impressionists were fascinated by moving light and pulsing air, Degas focused on the movements of man and animal. His first sketches

Laundresses Carrying Linen, 1885-1895
Charcoal, 17" × 23" (43.2 × 58.4 cm)
The Armand Hammer Collection, Los Angeles, California

The Dancer Jules Perrot, ca 1875
Charcoal and black chalk on pinkish laid paper
18⁹/₁₆" × 12⁵/₁₆" (47 × 31.2 cm)
The Syndics of the Fitzwilliam Museum
Cambridge, Great Britain

of racecourses date back to the beginning of the 1860s. At first he was interested in the jockeys, but he also turned a keen eye on the spectators. This led to such charming works as *Carriage at the Races* (see page 62), where the carriage is boldly put into the lower right-hand corner of the picture and is partly outside the picture. The people in the carriage are caught in their fashionable elegance, and the tender

Dancer in Profile Facing Right, ca 1874
Charcoal, black chalk, and white chalk on
beige-pink laid paper, 18⅛" × 12" (46.2 × 30.6 cm)
Cabinet des Dessins, Musée du Louvre, Paris

THE DANCE CLASS, ca 1874. Oil on canvas, 33½″ × 29½″ (85 × 75 cm). Musée d'Orsay, Paris

A Coryphée Resting, 1880-1882
Pastel on gray paper, 18¼" × 24⅛" (46.4 × 61.3 cm)
The Philadelphia Museum of Art. The John G. Johnson Collection

scene of the women and the child strike an intimate note foreshadowing the work of Vuillard. The carriage in the foreground contrasts with the flat expanse of fields behind it, in which scattered riders and another carriage emphasize the feeling of wide open space. The cool green of the spring landscape and the bluish-gray sky are quite different from Monet's contemporary studies of light. The wonderful light in this painting is created by a subtle and Corot-like harmony of color combined with a strong design.

Degas never tires of the theme of the racecourse. On September 27, 1881, the newspaper "Le Globe" started publishing Major Muybridge's photographs of a galloping horse, and Degas used them for his sketches. The photographs showed that traditional English prints were inaccurate when depicting galloping horses with their front legs outstretched. This is how Degas painted the horses racing in the background of *Carriage at the Races* (ca 1872). A later picture, such as *Before the Races* (see page 71), dated 1878-1880, is a striking example of Degas's ability to capture a split moment in a movement, in a fleeting image highlighted by the asymmetrical composition and the lack of perspective. Another painting of the same period, *At the Races* (see page 63), features a composition very similar to that of *Carriage at the Races*. In both paintings the figures are grouped in the lower right-hand corner of the paintings, cut off by the corner of the frame. But the emphasis on realistic drawing, which is evident in the earlier work, is replaced here by an arrangement of broad patches of color. Degas is still attracted by the nervous elegance and disciplined dancing grace of the horses, but everything is blended in a harmony of colors, which turns the canvas into a mosaic. People,

Dancer Adjusting Her Slipper, ca 1874
Pencil, charcoal, and white chalk on faded pink paper
12⅞″ × 9⅝″ (32.7 × 24.5 cm)
The Metropolitan Museum of Art, New York
Bequest of Mrs. H.O. Havemeyer

A Ballet Dancer in Position, 1874
Pencil with crayon and white chalk on pink paper
16⅛″ × 11¼″ (41 × 28.5 cm)
The Fogg Art Museum, Cambridge, Massachusetts
Bequest of Meta and Paul J. Sachs

animals, and landscape are combined into a decorative frieze, foreshadowing Degas's later work.

In the fall of 1872, Degas traveled to America with his brother René, in order to visit two other brothers who had settled as cotton traders in New Orleans. The journey was a welcome relief to the artist after the Franco-Prussian war, in which he had served in the artillery of the National Guard during the siege of Paris. He was not alone in this desire to leave France for a while after troubled times — Duret, Manet, Berthe Morisot, and Monet also went abroad in these post-war

THE MANTE FAMILY, ca 1884.   Pastel on paper, 35⁷⁄₁₆″ × 19¹¹⁄₁₆″ (90 × 50 cm)
Collection David Nahmad, New York

years. Degas remained in America until April 1873. His letters show that he found the exoticism of New Orleans's "colonial" society very attractive, but he also realized that he needed the challenging atmosphere of Paris to be a creative artist. He came to the conclusion that he could be inspired only by things familiar.

> I want nothing but my own little corner of the world, and I shall devote myself to it. Art does not expand, it distills itself. And, if you want comparisons at all costs, I would tell you that to produce good fruit one must be trained on a trellis. Like a wall tree the artist must remain thus all his life, arms extended, mouth open, assimilating everything that passes by and living by everything that surrounds him. [1]

The stay in New Orleans was not very productive, therefore. Apart from a few portraits of relatives, Degas painted only one major work there, *The Cotton Exchange in New Orleans* (see page 17), and this was the first painting, incidentally, to be bought by a museum (in 1878, by the Museum of Fine Arts in the French town of Pau). This is a painting of interiors, revealing a new and very elaborate approach to group portraits. The artist's uncle, Monsieur Musson, sits in the foreground, wearing a top-hat and testing cotton samples. René de Gas sits behind him, reading a newspaper, while the other brother, Achille, leans on the frame of a glass partition on the left. The problem of depicting

Three Studies of a Dancer, ca 1878
Black chalk heightened
with white on pink paper
Private collection

(1) Letter to Lorentz Frölich, Nov. 27, 1872. In Edgard Germain Hilaire Degas, *Lettres*. Ed. by Marcel Guérin, Introduction by Daniel Halévy. Paris: B. Grasset, 1931, p. 4.

The Little Fourteen-Year-Old Dancer, 1881
Wax, wire, fabric, and horse hair, h. 39" (99 cm)
Musée d'Orsay, Paris

contemporary material, an account of everyday business activity, is brilliantly resolved here. The office has an air of anonymous simplicity and coolness. There is a restraint, an absence of superfluous detail, which was to characterize Degas's paintings of dance classes. The interior is neutral to the point of resembling a public square, where the figures of the customers and traders, clerks and accountants, are captured sitting, standing, or walking about, as little aware of one another as passers-by on a square. The color scheme is simple and muted: dull browns, grays, and ochres predominate. The tight design and clear lines create an impression of bustle, with a precision that is far beyond anything a camera can do. *The Cotton Exchange in New Orleans* is one of Degas's most magnificent and mature works in his naturalistic style.

It is interesting that, after he found a source of inspiration in the sporting world of the turf, Degas should turn toward the stage and the ballet with an even greater insistence. These seemingly different themes, however, have one major element in common, movement. They both allowed Degas to explore that which interested him the most: a body in motion. Valéry may have referred to Degas when he compared, with a degree of coyness, a racehorse to a ballerina.

A horse walks on its toes. Four hoofs, like toenails, support it. No animal is closer to a "première danseuse", a star of the corps de ballet, than a perfectly balanced thoroughbred, as it seems to pause in flight under the hand of its rider, and then trips forward in the bright sunshine.[1]

Degas had a passion for the world of music and opera and his paintings of the stage broke new ground. In the eighteenth century, Antoine Watteau had found his inspiration in characters of the Commedia dell'Arte, and the theater became an accepted theme for serious painting. However, his pictures, and those of his successors, used the stage mainly as a background, a pretext for a sumptuous setting. Watteau and Tiepolo painted isolated figures of the Commedia dell'Arte as melancholy symbols of man's destiny, whereas Degas turned an unblinking gaze on the stage for its own sake. He was able to capture characteristic details and created snapshots of the ephemeral.

Four Studies of a Dancer, 1878-1879
Charcoal and white chalk on rose-beige wove paper
19¼" × 12⅝" (49.1 × 32 cm)
Cabinet des Dessins, Musée du Louvre, Paris

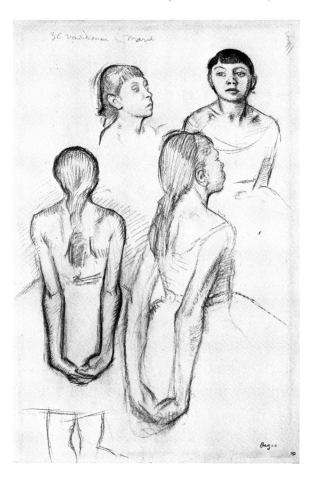

His first paintings from the theater were portraits. The earliest among such works, *Mademoiselle Fiocre in the Ballet "La Source"*, was a portrait of the ballerina in performance. In *The Orchestra at the Opera* (see page 30), Degas portrayed a number of musicians seated in the orchestra pit, among them such friends as the composer Emmanuel Chabrier, the flautist Joseph-Henri Altès, the cellist Pillet, the first violonist Lancien, the violist Gouffé, and the bassoonist Désiré Dihau. There are other versions and many preparatory studies for this picture, which is an excellent example of the goal he had set himself of portraying people in a public setting.

(1) Paul Valéry, *op. cit.*, p. 40.

Dancer, Fourth Position Front, on the Left Leg
1882-1895
Brown wax, h. 22⅝" (57.5 cm)
Collection: Mr. and Mrs. Paul Mellon
Upperville, Virginia

Upon his return from America, Degas immersed himself in a world he had missed very much when he was away. This was also a major turning point, because he no longer depicted only that which the audience or musicians could see of the stage. He went backstage. He became a cool observer of rehearsals.

The stage changed from being an incidental setting of the picture to become the theme of the picture itself. In *The Dance Lesson* and *The Dance Class* (see page 32), the ballerinas move in a space which is neither static nor enclosed. Only a corner of a long, stark room is represented, where the young ballet students perform their repetitive, almost ritual, exercise. The girls stand along the wall, listening to the ballet master and the violonist. They are exquisitely graceful. Their posture and movement range from total relaxation to extreme tension, recorded with almost fanatical verisimilitude.

The arrangement of the figures in the room is carried out with utmost precision; the chairs and desks are rhythmically related to the fairylike dancers. Degas is a master in the art of making space alive, of capturing the attention. He makes the room's very emptiness ring. This has been recognized by no one better than Max Liebermann, who says of Degas, "His compositions are not only done within a space, but also with this space. They are often simply determined by the distance from one object to another."[1] He painted all these pictures

(1) Max Liebermann. *Gesammelte Schriften*, Berlin, 1922, p. 77.

after small drawings sketched in his notebooks during dance lessons. In this respect he differs clearly from the other Impressionists; as John Rewald put it, Degas did not paint when observing, and he did not observe when painting. [1]

Following Degas's works showing the rehearsal room and the stage as a whole (even when only a corner is depicted), there came his series of astounding variations on the theme of dancers, in groups or isolated, in which the artist gained more and more freedom of vision, forever changing angles and capturing the ballerinas in the most surprising positions. The dancers are painted more and more in close-up. They do not move within a well defined three-dimensional space; they fill the foreground with colors against the wings and curtains. The most remarkable among these works are the different versions of *Ballet Dancer with a Bouquet, Curtsying* [2] (ca 1878). The ballerina is a sylph, arms outstretched, and still carried by the last movement at the close of her solo. She bows, bathed in the brilliant spotlight, with the unreal, fantastic, decor of the ballet as her background. She embodies the words of a sonnet by Degas himself: "[She] poises and balances [her] flight and weight." [3] Innumerable sketches and detailed studies were needed to achieve this effect of weightlessness. Degas emphasized this when he wrote, "There is no art less spontaneous than mine. What I do is the result of reflexion and the study of the great masters. I do not know the meaning of such words as inspiration, spontaneity, and artistic temperament. [4] ... It is essential to do the same subject again, ten times, a hundred times. Nothing in art must seem to be chance — not even movement." [5]

Horse with Jockey:
Horse Galloping on the Right Foot, 1865-1881
Brown wax, h. 9⅜" (23.8 cm)
Collection: Mr. and Mrs. Paul Mellon
Upperville, Virginia

(1) John Rewald. *op. cit.*
(2) Musée d'Orsay, Paris.
(3) Equilibre, balance et ton vol et ton poids.
(4) Paul André Lemoisne, *op. cit.*, p. 117.
(5) Letter to Bartholomé, January 17, 1886. In Edgard Hilaire Germain Degas, *op. cit.*, p. 107.

CARRIAGE AT THE RACES, ca 1872
Oil on canvas, 13¾″ × 21½″ (35 × 54.3 cm)
The Museum of Fine Arts, Boston
Arthur Gordon Tompkins Residuary Fund

AT THE RACES, 1877-1880
Oil on canvas
26³⁄₁₆″ × 32¼″ (66 × 81 cm)
Musée d'Orsay, Paris

His later paintings of dancers remove the figures completely from the realist atmosphere of the stage. The luminous tracery of colors, like fireworks, now reigns supreme. The dancers become the essence of rhythmic movement, pure emanations of colors. Dance is not shown any more as a performance requiring arduous practice, an ordinary expression of life, or an obvious display of beauty; it has become a solemn and mysterious ritual.

Between 1875 and 1880, Degas often went to the music hall, where he sensed more than anywhere else the pulsing life of the large city. *Music Hall (Les Ambassadeurs)*[1] may be the best of the works on this theme. It is a powerful evocation of the magical world and tinselly glamour of a music hall, a breathtaking grand finale of artificial lights and superimposed brilliant visions. *Women at the Terrace of a Café* (see page 42) is on a similar theme, but without the sumptuousness and the gay spirit. One looks out from the café onto the boulevard at night, out into a lonely night in the town, as someone passes by as a dark shadow. Prostitutes sit in the foreground, waiting for customers, with bored resignation and professional patience. Here Degas pushes the painting of interior to its limits. The interior he depicts is no more enclosed and intimate; it is a space open to the outside and the street, with — not surprisingly — the figures of two homeless

(1) Musée des Beaux-Art, Lyons.

Dancers at the Bar, 1876-1877
Oil with turpentine
and sepia on green paper
18⅞" × 24¹³⁄₁₆" (48 × 63 cm)
The British Museum, London

▷

Two Dancers at the Bar
ca 1877-1879
Pastel on paper
26‴ × 20⅛" (66 × 51 cm)
Private collection, U.S.A.
Courtesy Acquavella Galleries
New York

THE GREEN DANCERS, 1877-1879. Pastel and gouache, 26″ × 14⅛″ (66 × 36 cm)
Collection Thyssen-Bornemisza, Lugano

DANCERS IN THE WINGS, ca 1880.   Pastel and tempera on paper, 27¼″ × 19¾″ (69.2 × 50.2 cm)
Norton Simon Art Foundation, Pasadena, California

FOUR DANCERS, ca 1899
Oil on canvas, 59½″ × 71″ (151 × 180 cm)
National Gallery of Art, Washington, D.C.
The Chester Dale Collection

DANCERS PREPARING FOR
THE BALLET, ca 1875
Oil on canvas
29³⁄₁₆″ × 23¾″ (74.1 × 60.5 cm)
The Art Institute of Chicago
Gift of Mr. and Mrs. Gordon Palmer
Mrs. Bertha P. Thorne
Mr. and Mrs. Arthur M. Wood
and Mrs. Rose M. Palmer

social outcasts. *The Absinth Drinkers* (see page 43), belongs to the same series. It contains an element of social criticism, similar to that in Zola's "L'Assommoir" denouncing the destruction caused by alcoholism. But it also conveys an anguished image of man's existence. The last two customers at the café are seated in the right-hand part of the painting, with the gray reflection of the street behind them. The couple is surrounded by emptiness. The actress Ellen Andrée and the engraver Marcellin Desboutin served as models, but the painting goes beyond a mere portrait. They become the symbol of a nameless destiny. Gotthard Jadlicka described the abyss of hopelessness in *The Absinth Drinkers* most vividly:

> This picture makes loneliness and emptiness tangible. In no other European painting does this feeling appear with such intensity. The atmosphere created here is the very opposite of the mixture of well-being and self-confidence which can be seen in works by other Impressionists. The mood which Degas wanted, indeed, needed to capture, is of two frightened people who seek each other's company, which in turn increases their painful feeling of loneliness.[1]

The Rape (see page 45) conveys a similar atmosphere. The name of the painting may be misleading. It probably refers to a scene in Zola's novel, "Madeleine Férat," in which Madeleine says to Francis that he is tormented because he loves her and she cannot be his. But it also evokes the theme of the war between man and woman, which was to become dominant at the end of the nineteenth century, especially in the works of Toulouse-Lautrec and Edvard Munch.

Women at the Terrace of a Café, The Absinth Drinkers, The Rape as well as several paintings set in a brothel, have a social content which can also be found in paintings Degas made of the working class. He was not interested in the bohemian life, which always includes a hint of Romanticism. He took up themes treated earlier by Honoré Daumier and painted women ironing, washerwomen, milliners. Daumier's working man, however, was a heroic, almost mythical, figure. Unsentimental but loving, Daumier felt a deep compassion for the worker, whose

---

(1) Gotthard Jedlicka. "Degas L'Absinthe", in *Pariser Tagebuch*, Frankfurt, 1953.

JOCKEYS IN THE RAIN, 1880-1881
Pastel, 18⅛″ × 21¹¹⁄₁₆″ (46 × 55 cm)
Glasgow Art Gallery and Museum

BEFORE THE RACE, 1880
Pastel on paper, 19¾″ × 24¾″ (50 × 63 cm)
Private collection, U.S.A.
Courtesy Acquavella Galleries, New York

Portrait of Madame Ernest May, 1881
Black chalk with highlights in pastel
11¹³⁄₁₆″ × 9¼″ (30 × 23.5 cm)
Private collection, San Francisco

greatness could not be destroyed by poverty. Degas, on the other hand, saw no heroism in everyday modern work. His *Ironers* (see page 46) are of frightening ugliness. Their work is dull. The straining effort of the woman on the right contrasts with the brief repose of the woman on the left. One is bent forward to put her weight and strength in a pressing movement on the iron, while the other yawns and raises one arm to stretch her tired body — her wide-open mouth a cameo of disenchanting vulgarity. These working women are portrayed as harridans. The paintings of the milliners (see page 47) show less of a tendency to make the women ugly. The milliners are nevertheless caught in the most absurd positions, surrounded by brightly colored hats and slanting mirrors often placed at the edge of the painting. They are completely absorbed by the fitting of hats and lose all individual dignity. Their clothing, their behavior, their charm as women must be toned down.

After 1880 Degas also explored the theme of women bathing. French artists devoted a significant part of their work to the praise of woman's beauty, albeit less in the nineteenth than in the eighteenth century. Suffice it to mention Manet's glorious Parisians and Renoir's women. There is no trace of loving homage in Degas, nor is he influenced by Ingres's heathen cult of the female body or by Théodore Chassériau's voluptuous happiness. Degas describes intimate scenes without intimacy, bodies without sensuality. As he himself noted, he painted women "as an animal grooming itself, a cat licking itself."[1]

(1) Paul André Lemoisne, *op. cit.*, p. 118.

SIX FRIENDS OF THE ARTIST, 1885
Pastel and black chalk on gray paper now yellowed, 45¼″ × 28″ (113 × 70 cm)
Museum of Art, Rhode Island School of Design, Providence

Study of a Nude, ca 1890-1895
Pastel and charcoal
24⅜″ × 18⅞″ (62 × 48 cm)
Private collection

Bather, ca 1890
Charcoal on white paper
23½″ × 18″ (60 × 46 cm)
Private collection

The women bathing, washing, drying themselves, combing their hair or having it combed, are mainly seen from behind. They do not seem to heed the intimacy of the boudoir or bathroom scene. The viewer intrudes on these women's privacy, subjecting them to a detached, almost cruel, scrutiny. It is as if the artist were watching them through a keyhole, catching a glimpse of a naked body, an often distorted posture, as it would otherwise be seen perhaps only by a doctor examining a patient.[1] This matter-of-fact depiction of woman was bound to be criticized by Degas's contemporaries. The critic J.-K. Huysmans accused him, with some irony, of having dealt a deadly blow to nineteenth-century painting by bringing

(1) Fritz Laufer, *Das Interieur in der Malerei des 19. Jahrhunderts*, unpublished doctoral thesis, 1952.

Woman by a Fireplace, ca 1879-1880. Monotype on laid paper, 10⅞″ × 14⅞″ (27.5 × 37.7 cm)
National Gallery of Art, Washington, D.C. Collection Mr. and Mrs. Paul Mellon

WOMAN IN BATH, 1883
Pastel, 12¼″ × 11″ (31 × 28 cm)
Private collection
Courtesy Galerie Schmit, Paris

A WOMAN HAVING HER HAIR COMBED, 1886
Pastel on paper, 29⅛″ × 23⅞″ (74 × 60.6 cm)
The Metropolitan Museum of Art, New York
Bequest of Mrs. H.O. Havemeyer

▷

THE TUB, 1886
Pastel on paper, 26″ × 23⅝″ (60 × 83 cm)
Musée d'Orsay, Paris

Woman in Bath, ca 1892
Oil on canvas, 28½″ × 35¾″ (72.4 × 90.8 cm)
Art Gallery of Ontario, Toronto
Frank P. Wood Endowment

Woman Seated, Drying Herself, ca 1894
Pastel, 26⅜″ × 33⅞″ (67 × 86 cm)
Musée d'Art et d'Histoire, Neuchâtel, Switzerland
Bequest of Yvan and Hélène Amez-Droz

down to earth the last idol. In point of fact Degas had no intention of humiliating or exposing women. In *A Woman Having Her Hair Combed* (see page 77), a woman offers the radiating beauty of her body to the light in a wonderfully balanced composition. Most of all, Degas is interested in depicting on the canvas a body in motion. His paintings and drawings of bathing women become a complete repertoire of every posture and movement of a woman in her bathroom.

Finally, the leading thread in all of Degas's works, whether paintings of jockeys, dancers, working women, or women bathing, is that he always depicts an anonymous person caught in a movement characteristic of a particular situation or occupation. He does not paint a body as it happens to move, he paints the shape of a movement in a body. His figures are not that of complex and unique individuals rich in existential choices; they are entirely defined by one situation, so that they are mostly anonymous.

Degas's technique underlines this approach to the human figure. Like the other Impressionists, he uses a naturalistic perspective, but one which is pushed to its limits by severe

Woman Drying Herself, ca 1903
Charcoal with highlights in reddish brown chalk
27¹⁵/₁₆″ × 27¹⁵/₁₆″ (71 × 71 cm)
Collection David Nahmad, New York

Woman Drying Her Hair, ca 1895-1902
Charcoal, 28¼″ × 27⅛″ (71.7 × 68.9 cm)
Private Collection, U.S.A.
Courtesy Acquavella Galleries, New York

NUDE STEPPING INTO A BATHTUB, 1895-1900
Pastel, 11⅜″ × 9⅞″ (29 × 25 cm)
National Museum of Wales, Cardiff

foreshortenings and sharp slanting lines. As a result he achieves a new sense of space, defined by an unusual angle, in which a figure is caught in motion, and this new sense of space was to exert a strong influence on the art of the twentieth century. His paintings are an intricate arrangement of overlapping levels, with a deep perspective and fragmented angles; they are like snapshots taken with an unfailing hand. While this sense of space is strongly emphasized, Degas also uses wide expanses of pure color which may be derived from the art of Japanese prints. Bracquemond had discovered Hokusai's woodcuts in 1956. Fascination with Japanese art was to reach its zenith with Gauguin, Van Gogh, Toulouse-Lautrec, Pierre Bonnard, and Vuillard. Before them, Degas had been the first to be deeply impressed by the graphic style and subtle line of Japanese woodcuts, their off-center arrangements and foreshortenings.

It has been said that light is the Impressionists' main theme.[1] From being an element of accuracy in naturalistic landscape paintings, light became the most important component, and particular figures and objects became less significant than the atmosphere created by a vibration of separate brushstrokes. Degas never used this impressionistic technique. Far into the 1870s he continued to paint dark gray shadows. Furthermore, he always emphasized sketches as a necessary step to capture movement. "The dancer is for me only an excuse to draw..." Degas said "Drawing is not the same as form, but a way of seeing form."[2] Drawing is the foundation

Woman Standing in a Bathtub
ca 1895-1900
Charcoal on yellow tracing paper
17⅛″ × 11⅝″ (43.5 × 29.5 cm)
The Sterling and Francine Clark Institute
Williamstown, Massachusetts

(1) Fritz Novotny. *Die grossen französischen Impressionisten*, Vienna, 1952, p. 13.
(2) Paul Valéry, *op. cit.*, p. 82.

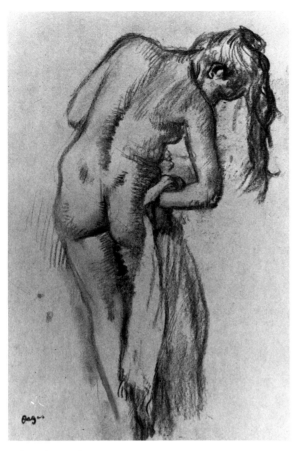

After the Bath
ca 1895-1900
Charcoal on yellow tracing paper
14¹⁄₁₆″ × 9¹⁵⁄₁₆″ (35.7 × 25.2 cm)
The Sterling and Francine Clark Institute
Williamstown, Massachusetts

of Degas's art and it remains strong under impressionistic irridescent colors and blurred figures.

Around 1880 his grays grave way to brilliant colors, ranging from red to russet, and muted tones were replaced by warm ones. This came with a change in style and technique, in which pastels became Degas's dominant medium. The switch to pastels had been progressive. Degas used them only rarely before 1869. His first large works in pastel date from around 1875-1876. After 1880-1886 he almost completely abandoned oil painting, unless he could apply and blend the colors to reproduce the brilliant qualities of pastel pigments, as in *Portrait of a Woman with a Red Shawl* (1886)[1] or *Four Dancers* (see page 68). Manet and Renoir also used pastels on occasion, but Degas was the only nineteenth-century painter who made them his primary medium, calling to mind the great pastel period of the eighteenth century. He saw that pastels struck a balance between painting and drawing, enabling him to paint while drawing. Furthermore, he expanded the possibilities offered by pastels by combining them with gouache, watercolor, oils mixed freely with turpentine, and even monotypes. Colors are applied in vigorous parallel hatchings. A shimmering blending of tones is achieved by superimposed layers of pigments — each layer separately coated with fixative between applications of pastel strokes — which create a surface built up of streaks of pure color as well as an impression of transparency. This technique goes beyond the rough textured canvases of Monet

(1) Emil G. Buehrle Foundation, Zurich.

84

or the fractured colors of Pointillism. Degas was able to turn away from a naturalistic rendering of space and produce, in his later pastels, a hazy swirl of brilliant colors. Gone are the dark tones and the preoccupation with space. Hatchings and spots create a lustrous dance of color. Lines become boundaries between flows of color that simplify to the limit both body and space. This does not mean, however, that the movement of the ballerinas and the bathing women are not captured as accurately as they were before. But gesture does not express character, personality, or class anymore; it expresses form, line, and balance. These sharply observed movements, combined with an unending flare of colors, turn the later works into fantastic visions. They are experiments in the abstract relationship between lines and forms, light and color, to the exclusion of the narrative content. Herein lies the modern quality in these later pastels, foreshadowing twentieth-century art, and Fauvism in particular.

There is little to say about Degas's life. Upon his return from America, he sought out the group of painters who were to form the Impressionist group and he took part in the group's first exhibition in 1874. He continued to exhibit with them, in spite of his open criticism of the narrow Impressionist credo. He himself said, "I always tried to urge my colleagues to seek for new combinations along the path of draftsmanship, which I consider a more fruitful field than color. But they wouldn't listen to me, and have gone the other way." [1]

In 1874 his father died, leaving the bank in a difficult financial situation. In the following years his brothers suffered

Half-Length Nude Girl, ca 1895
Charcoal heightened with white on tracing paper
21¼" × 15¼" (53.9 × 38.8 cm)
The Syndics of the Fitzwilliam Museum
Cambridge, Great Britain

(1) Walter Sickert, "Edgar Degas", in *Burlington Magazine*, November 1917, p. 184.

85

additional heavy losses owing to poor management. Degas sold a part of his private art collection in order to help them avoid possible bankruptcy — this distressed him very much, and he regarded this financial setback as a blight on the family honor. He remained, however, an avid art collector of sure taste. For a time he thought of bequeathing his entire collection to the French state, but he dismissed the idea after Gustave Moreau's bequest of his studio. Degas's collection was auctioned off after his death; among the paintings he owned were two by El Greco, one by Albert Cuyp, and, above

Group of Dancers, 1899
Pastel, 20⅛" × 18⅞" (51 × 48 cm)
Private collection

A Dancer Adjusting Her Shoulder Strap, ca 1895
Pastel over charcoal drawing on tracing paper
18¾" × 14½" (47.5 × 37 cm)
Kunsthalle Bremen, Federal Republic of Germany

all, pictures by Ingres, Delacroix, Corot, Cézanne, Manet, Cassatt, Pissarro, Sisley, Renoir, Gauguin, Van Gogh, as well as works by such close friends as Bartholomé.

Degas's eyesight began to falter in 1871 and worsened after 1893. Nevertheless, he continued to travel a great deal. In 1886, he went to Naples. In 1889 he went with Giovanni Boldini to Spain and Morocco. In 1890 he went with Bartholomé to Burgundy. After 1898 he became progressively blind. Although painting was becoming difficult, his hand and spirit were still

87

alive. He worked on an increasingly large scale, applying pastels and charcoal with enormous boldness. Often he also traced another drawing on tracing paper or made a counterproof of a charcoal to be later developed into pastel. By 1908 he was no longer able to draw, and the following year he had to give up painting. Since 1880 he had experimented with sculpture and he modeled more and more as his eyesight declined, making sculptures of ballerinas and horses (see pages 58, 60 and 61).

After 1898 he led a solitary life. One after another, his friends died and finally, in 1912, he lost his most intimate friend, Henri Rouart. The same year, he had to leave his apartment and studio in the Rue Victor-Massé. Suzanne Valadon found another apartment for him on Boulevard Clichy, but the move distressed him and he never really settled in his new lodgings. In 1914, he had the satisfaction of seeing many of his most remarkable works receive their due recognition when the Camondo collection was bequeathed to the Louvre.

Dancer Fixing Her Shoe, ca 1885
Charcoal and white pastel on gray paper
17⅝" × 12¼" (43.2 × 29.4 cm)
Norton Simon Art Foundation
Pasadena, California

After he could no longer work, he wandered for hours, alone, through the streets of his beloved Paris. The last of his living friends, Bartholomé, took photographs of Degas in 1915, showing a figure resembling a blind Homer or King Lear, his features transformed by a tragic spiritual force. When he died on September 27, 1917, the world hardly took notice, immersed as it was in a world war. In itself, his personal life had been of little importance. It had been totally dedicated to an undying body of work.

BALLET REHEARSAL, ca 1891. Oil on canvas, 14⅛″ × 34½″ (36 × 87.5 cm)
Yale University Art Gallery, New Haven, Connecticut. Gift of Duncan Phillips

Dancer Adjusting Her Stocking
ca 1880
Charcoal and white chalk
9½″ × 12¼″ (24.2 × 31.3 cm)
The Syndics of
the Fitzwilliam Museum
Cambridge, Great Britain

FRIEZE OF DANCERS, ca 1883. Oil on canvas, 27¾" × 79" (70.5 × 200.8 cm)
The Cleveland Museum of Art, Ohio. Gift of the Hanna Fund

*We wish to thank the owners of the pictures reproduced herein, as well as those collectors who did not want to have their name mentioned.
Our special thanks to the Galerie Schmit in Paris and the Acquavella Galleries in New York for their help.*

CANADA: Art Gallery of Ontario, *Toronto.*

FRANCE: Bibliothèque nationale, *Paris* - Cabinet des Dessins, Louvre, *Paris* - Musée d'Orsay, *Paris* - Musée
                                        des Beaux-Arts, *Pau.*

UNITED KINGDOM: The Barber Institute of Fine Arts, *Birmingham* - Fitzwilliam Museum, *Cambridge* - National
                                        Museum of Wales, *Cardiff* - *Glasgow* Art Gallery and Museum - The British Museum, *London* -
                                        The National Gallery, *London.*

FEDERAL REPUBLIC OF GERMANY: Kunsthalle, *Bremen* - Städelsches Kunstinstitut, *Frankfurt.*

SWITZERLAND: Musée d'Art et d'Histoire, *Neuchâtel* - Collection Thyssen-Bornemisza, *Lugano* - Stiftung
                                        Sammlung E.G. Bührle, *Zurich.*

U.S.A.:   The Museum of Fine Arts, *Boston* - The Fogg Art Museum, *Cambridge, Mass.* - The Art Institute,
                                        Chicago - The *Cleveland* Museum of Art - The Wadsworth Atheneum, *Hartford, Conn.* - The
                                        Nelson Atkins Museum, *Kansas City* - The Armand Hammer Collection, *Los Angeles* - The
                                        Minneapolis Institute of Arts - Yale University Art Gallery, *New Haven, Conn.* - The Brooklyn
                                        Museum, *New York* - The Metropolitan Museum of Art, *New York* - Mr. David Nahmad,
                                        New York - Mr. and Mrs. E.V. Thaw, *New York* - Smith College of Art, *Northampton, Mass.* -
                                        Norton Simon Art Foundation, *Pasadena* - The *Philadelphia* Museum of Art - Museum of Art,
                                        Rhode Island School of Design, *Providence* - The *Toledo* Museum of Art, Ohio - Mr. and Mrs.
                                        Paul Mellon, *Upperville, Va.* - The Corcoran Gallery of Art, *Washington D.C.* - National Gallery
                                        of Art, *Washington, D.C.* - The Sterling and Francine Clark Institute, *Williamstown, Mass.*

PHOTOGRAPHS

Larry Ostrom, Toronto - Service Photographique de la Réunion des Musées Nationaux, Paris - Artothek, Planegg/Munich - Walter Dräyer,
Zurich - Joseph Szaszfai, Hartford, Conn. - Richard W. Caspole, New Haven, Conn. - Bruce C. Jones, Centerport, New York - Eric Pollitzer,
Hempstead, New York - Otto Nelson, New York.

Rehearsal of the Dance.   Charcoal, 21¾″ × 40½″ (55.8 × 103 cm)
The Nelson-Atkins Museum of Art, Kansas City, Missouri. Nelson Fund. Gift from Harold Woodbury Parsons

Dancers at the Bar, ca 1905
Charcoal and pastel on tracing paper mounted on wove paper, 18¼″ × 40‴ (46.4 × 101.6 cm)
The Toledo Museum of Art, Ohio. Gift of Mrs. C. Lockhart McKelvy

THE REHEARSAL ROOM, 1889-1905. Oil on canvas, 16¼″ × 36¼″ (41.5 × 92 cm)
Foundation Emil G. Bührle, Zurich

BIOGRAPHY

1834   July 19, Hilaire-Germain-Edgar de Gas born at 8 Rue Saint-Georges in Paris, the eldest son of a wealthy Neapolitan-born banker, Augustin de Gas and Célestine Musson, a Creole from New Orleans. His father was interested in the arts and loved music. Eventually, he allowed his son to devote himself to becoming an artist.

1845-53   Attended the Lycée Louis-le-Grand, where he became friends with Henri Rouart, Paul Valpinçon, and Ludovic Halévy.

1847   His mother died.

1852   Through his cultured father, he made the acquaintance of some important collectors of his time (Edouard Valpinçon, Prince Gregorio Soutzo, Louis Lacaze) as well as many professional musicians.

1853   Began reading law.

1853-55   Took lessons with the painter Barrias, then studied with Louis Lamothe, a pupil of Ingres. Lamothe introduced him to the Ecole des Beaux-Arts.

1855   Made a journey to Lyons and the south of France. Through his friends the Valpinçons, he had a brief but memorable meeting with Ingres.

1856-59   His first trip to Italy: Naples, where his paternal grandfather lived; Rome; Florence, where his aunt, Baroness Bellelli, and cousins lived. Starts on the portrait of *The Bellelli Family*. He studied the early Renaissance masters and, in Florence, met the painters known as the Macchiaioli (Café Michelangelo).

1860-61   Portaits and history paintings. *Young Spartans Exercising*, *The Daughter of Jephthah*. First studies of horses and riders.

1861-63   Became a friend of Duranty, the champion of Realism.

1862   Beginning of a long-standing friendship with Manet, whom he met at the Louvre. Through Manet he made the acquaintance of Renoir, Monet, and Zola. Meetings at the Café de Bade, then at the Café Guerbois, near the Place Clichy.

1864   Several portraits of Manet.

1865   First entry at the Salon, *The Misfortunes of the City of Orléans*, which earned him compliments from Puvis de Chavannes. Began to sign his name "Degas." Marriage of his sister Marguerite to Henri Fèvre, an architect.

1865-70   Series of portraits, first of isolated figures, then of groups.

1866   Exhibited *The Steeplechase*, or *The Wounded Jockey*, at the Salon.

1867   Two portraits at the Salon, which were favorably reviewed by Castagnary.

1868   First paintings of dancers. *Mademoiselle Fiocre* at the Salon.

1869   Pastel landscapes painted in the open air. Trip to Italy. *Portrait of Madame G.* at the Salon. His brother René married their blind, widowed cousin, Estelle Musson Balfour, in New Orleans. David Balfour had been killed during the Civil War. First paintings on the theme of the laundress.

1870   Last entry at the Salon, *Portrait of Madame Camus*.

1870-72   Served in the National Guard in Paris during the war. Was in Normandy during the Commune. His eyesight was beginning to falter and he had to avoid painting in a bright light. First paintings of dancers.

1872   Met Durand-Ruel.

1872-73   Made a journey to New Orleans. *The Cotton Exchange in New Orleans*.

1873   Made a short trip to Italy.

1874   His father died.
Contributed ten works to the first Impressionist exhibition. Baritone Jean Baptiste Faure bougt *The Dancing Class*.

1875   Made a trip to Italy: Naples, Florence, Pisa, and Genoa.

1876   Contributed twenty-four works to the second Impressionist exhibition, including *The Absinth Drinkers* and *The Ironers*. Paintings on the theme of the "café-concert."
Sold his collection of paintings to help the family avoid bankruptcy. He gave most of his assets to his brothers and began having serious financial difficulties. Started painting fans for commercial purposes.

1877   Third Impressionist exhibition, where he contributed twenty-two prints, drawings, monotypes, and paintings.

1878   The museum in Pau bought *The Cotton Exchange*. He began to use primarily pastels, in particular a technique which he had invented and called "distemper-pastel."

1879   Divorce of his brother René. Degas sided with his sister-in-law, and the relationship between the two brothers was to be strained for over ten years.
Fourth Impressionist exhibition: he contributed fans, portraits, and *Mademoiselle Lala at the Fernando Circus*.

1879-80   Exhibited prints together with Mary Cassatt and Camille Pissarro.

1880   Made a trip to Spain.
Fifth Impressionist exhibition: eight paintings and pastels, including *Portrait of Duranty*. "La Gazette des Beaux-Arts" published the first positive review of an Impressionist exhibition. First sculpture, *The Schoolgirl*.

1881-85   Publication of Muybridge's photographs.

1881   Sixth Impressionist exhibition: several pastels and an almost life-size wax sculpture, *Fourteen-Year-Old Dancer*.

1882   Degas and Mary Cassatt abstained from showing at the Impressionist exhibition. Several pastels on the theme of the milliner. He again took up the theme of the women ironing. First important works depicting a woman at her toilet.
Made a short trip to Spain and, later, stayed near Geneva.

1884   Spent summer in the country with the Valpinçons.

1885   Made a trip to Le Havre, the Mont Saint-Michel and Dieppe, where he met Gauguin.

1886   Made a trip to Naples in January. Last Impressionist exhibition, where he showed five oils and ten pastels, a series of women at their toilet. After this date he stopped exhibiting pictures, selling them on contract through Durand-Ruel.

1889   Made a trip to Spain and Morocco.

1890   Made a trip to Burgundy, from which he drew a series of landscapes on monotypes. Series of bathers and women combing their hair.

1892   Solo exhibition at Durand-Ruel. Death of his brother Achille.

1893-95   His eyesight worsened.

1895   His sister Marguerite died in Buenos-Aires.

1897   Made a trip to Mautauban in order to see Ingres' paintings.

1898-1908   Became progressively blind and led a solitary life.

1908   Unable to draw.

1909   Unable to paint.

1911   Death of Alexis Rouart.

1912   Had to leave his apartment on Rue Victor-Massé. Suzanne Valadon found another apartment for him on the Boulevard de Clichy, but the move made him unhappy and he never really settled in his new lodgings.
His best friend, Henri Rouart, died and his art collection was sold at an auction in December.

1917   Died on September 27 and was buried in the Montmartre cemetery.

1918   The Edgar Degas collection was auctioned off.

BIBLIOGRAPHY

ADHÉMAR, J. and CACHIN, F. *Degas, Gravures et monotypes*. Paris: Arts et Métiers graphiques, 1973. Munich, 1973. *Degas, Prints and Monotypes*. Tr. by Jane Brenton. New York: Viking, 1974. Munich, 1973.

ADRIANI, Gotz. *Edgar Degas: Pastelle, Ölskizzen, Zeichnungen*. Cologne: Dumont, 1984.

ANDRÉ, Albert. *Degas*. Paris, 1934.

BOGGS, Jean Sutherland. *Portraits by Degas*. Berkeley: University of California Press, 1962.

BOGGS, Jean Sutherland. *Drawings by Degas*. Saint Louis, 1966.

BOREL, P. *Les Sculptures inédites de Degas. Choix de cires originales*. Geneva: P. Cailler, 1949.

BOURET, Jean. *Degas*. Paris, 1965. Tr. by Daphne Woodward, London: Thames & Hudson, 1965.

BROWSE, Lillian. *Degas Dancers*. New York: Studio Publications, 1949.

CABANNE, Pierre. *Edgar Degas*. Paris: Pierre Tisné, 1957. Munich, 1960.

CHAMPIGNEULLE. *Degas: Dessins*. Paris: Ed. des Deux Mondes, 1952.

COOPER, Douglas. *Pastels*. New York: MacMillan, 1952.

COQUIOT, G. *Degas*. Paris: Ollendorf, 1924.

DEGAS, E. *Lettres*. Recueillies et annotées par M. Guérin. Préface de Daniel Halévy. Paris: B. Grasset, 1931, 1945. Ed. by M. Guérin, tr. by Marguerite Kay. Oxford : B. Cassirer, 1947. New York: Studio Publications, 1948.

DUFWA, Jacques. *Winds from the East: A Study in the Art of Manet, Degas, Monet and Whistler, 1856-86*. Stockholm: Almqvist & Wiskell; Atlantic Highlands, N.J.: Humanities Press, 1981.

DUNLOP Ian. *Degas*. London: Thames & Hudson, New York: Harper and Row, 1979.

FÈVRE, Jeanne. *Mon oncle Degas*. Geneva: P. Cailler, 1949.

FOSCA, François. *Degas*. Paris: A. Messein, 1921.

FOSCA, François. *Degas*. Tr. by James Emmons. Geneva: Skira, 1954.

GRABER, Hans. *Edgar Degas nach eigenen und fremden Zeugnissen*. Basel: Benno Schwabe, 1942.

GRAPPE, Georges. *Degas*. Paris: Plon, 1936.

GROWE, Berndt. *Zur Bildkonzeption E. Degas*. Frankfurt, 1981.

GUÉRIN, M. *Dix-neuf portraits de Degas*. Paris: M. Guerin, 1931.

HALÉVY, Daniel. *Degas parle*. Paris: La Palatine, 1960. *My Friend Degas*. Middletown, Conn.: Wesleyan University Press, 1964.

HAUSENSTEIN, Wilhelm. *Degas*. Berne: Alfred Schertz, 1948.

HEBERMANN, M. *Degas*. Berlin: Cassirer, 1899.

HERTZ, Henri. *Degas*. Paris: Félix Alcan, 1920.

HOPPE, H. *Degas*. Stockholm, 1922.

HUYGHE, René. *Edgar Hilaire Germain Degas*. Paris: Flammarion, 1953.

JAMOT, Paul. *Degas*. Paris: Gazette des Beaux-Arts, 1924.

JANIS, E. P. *Degas Monotypes. Catalogue raisonné*. Cambridge, Mass., 1968.

KEYSER, Eugenie de. *Degas: Réalité et métaphore*. Louvain-la-Neuve: Publications d'histoire de l'art et d'archéologie de l'Université catholique de Louvain, No. 25, 1981.

KOPPLIN, Monika. *Das Fächerblatt von Manet bis Kokoschka. Europaïsche Traditionen und japanische Einflüsse*. Saulgau, 1981.

KRESAK, Fedor. *Edgar Degas*. Prague, 1979.

LAFOND, Paul. *Degas*. Paris: H. Floury, 1918-19, 1922.

LASSAIGNE, Jacques. *Edgar Degas*. Paris, 1945.

LEFÉBURE, Amaury. *Degas*. Paris, 1981.

LEMOISNE, Paul André. *Degas et son œuvre*. Paris: Paul Brame & C.M. de Haucke, 1946; Plon, 1954.

LÉVÊQUE, Jean-Jacques. *Edgar Degas*. Paris: Siloé, 1978.

LEYMARIE, Jean. *Les Dessins d'Edgar Degas*. Paris: Hazan, 1948, 1953.

LIEBERMANN, M. *Degas*. Berlin, 1899, 1912.

LIPTON, Eunice. *Looking into Degas: Uneasy Images of Women and Modern Life*. Berkeley, California: University of California Press, 1986.

LONGSTREET, Stephen. *The Drawings of Edgar Degas*. Los Angeles: Borden, 1964.

MANSON, J. *The Life and Work of Edgar Degas*. London: Studio Ltd., 1927.

MATT, Leonard von and REWALD, John. *Degas, Das plastische Werk*. Zurich: Manesse, 1957.

MAUCLAIR, Camille. *Degas*. Paris: Hypérion, 1937. New York: Hyperion, 1941.

McMULLEN, Roy. *Degas, His Life, Time, and Work*. Boston: Houghton Mifflin, 1984.

MEHRING, Walter. *Hilaire Germain Edgar Degas, 1834-1917. Thirty Drawings and Pastels*. New York: Herrmann, 1944.

MEIER-GRAEFE, Julius. *Degas. Ein Beitrag zur Entwicklungsgeschichte der modernen Malerei*. Munich: R. Piper, 1920. *Degas*. Tr. by J. Holroyd Reece. London: E. Benn Ltd., 1923, 1927.

MILLARD, Charles W. *The Sculpture of Edgar Degas*. Princeton, N.J.: Princeton University Press, 1976.

MINERVINO, Fiorella. *L'Opera completa di Degas*. Milan: Rizzoli, 1970.

MOORE, G. *Reminiscences of the Impressionist Painters*. Dublin, 1906.

NICODEMI, Giorgio. *Il pittore, i cavalli e le ballerine*. Milan: Bietti, 1945.

PECIRKA, Jaromir. *Edgar Degas, Zeichnungen*. Prague, 1963. *Drawings of Edgar Degas*. London: Peter Neville, 1963.

POOL, Phoebe. *Degas*. New York: Malboro, 1963.

REBATET, Marguerite. *Degas*. Paris: P. Tisné, 1944.

REFF, Theodore. *Degas: The Artist's Mind*. New York: The Metropolitan Museum of Art & Harper and Row, 1976.

REFF, Theodore. *The Notebooks of Degas. A catalogue of the thirty-eight notebooks in the Bibliothèque nationale and other collections.* 2nd rev. ed. New York: Hacker Art Books, 1985.

REWALD, John. *Degas, Works in Sculpture. A complete catalogue.* Tr. by John Coleman and Noel Moulton. New York: Pantheon, 1944, 1956.

REWALD, John. *History of Impressionism.* New York: Museum of Modern Art, Fourth ed., 1980. Cologne: Dumont, 1965.

RICH, D.C. *Degas.* New York: Harry N. Abrams, 1951. Cologne: Dumont, 1959.

RICH, D.C. *Edgar Hilaire Germain Degas.* New York: Abrams, 1985.

RIVIÈRE, Georges. *Les Dessins de Degas.* Paris: Demotte, 1922-23.

RIVIÈRE, Georges. *M. Degas, bourgeois de Paris.* Paris: Floury, 1935.

ROBERTS, Keith. *Degas.* Rev., enl. ed. Oxford: Phaidon, 1982.

ROGER-MARX, Claude. *Degas, Pastels et Dessins.* Paris: D. Jacomet, 1957.

ROSENBERG, Jakob. *Great Draughtsmen from Pisanello to Picasso.* Cambridge, Mass.: Harvard, 1959.

ROUART, Denis. *Degas, à la recherche de sa technique.* Paris: Floury, 1945.

ROUART, Denis. *Degas. Dessins.* Paris: Braun, 1945.

ROUART, Denis. *Degas. Monotypes.* Paris, n.d. (1948).

SALMON, André. *Propos d'atelier.* Paris: Excelsior, 1938.

SCHWABE, Randolf. *Degas. The Draughtsman.* London: Art Trade Press, 1948.

SERULLAZ, Maurice. *L'Univers de Degas.* Paris: Screpel, 1979.

SHINODA, Yujiro. *Degas. Der Einzug des Japanischen in die französische Malerei.* Cologne: Dumont, 1957.

SUTTON, Denys. *Edgar Degas. Life and Work.* New York: Rizzoli, 1986.

TERRASSE, Antoine. *Degas et la photographie.* Paris: Denoël, 1983.

TUGENDKHOL'D, Ia. *Edgar Degas i ego iskusstvo.* Moscow : Z.J. Grschebin, 1922.

VALÉRY, Paul. *Degas, danse, dessin.* Paris: Vollard, 1936; Gallimard, 1938. New York, 1948.

VALÉRY, Paul. *Erinnerung an Degas.* Zurich, 1940.

VALÉRY, Paul. *Degas, Manet, Morisot.* Tr. by David Paul. Int. by Douglas Cooper. New York: Pantheon, 1960.

VANBESSELAERE, W. *Degas.* Brussels, 1941.

VOLLARD, Ambroise. *Degas.* Paris: Crès, 1924, 1938. *Degas, an Intimate Portrait.* Tr. by Randolph T. Weaver New York: Greenberg, 1927.

VOLLARD, Ambroise. *En écoutant Cézanne, Degas, Renoir.* Paris: Grasset, 1938.

WERNER, Alfred. *Degas. Pastels.* New York: Watson-Guptill, 1969.

ZERNOV, B. *Degas.* Moscow: Soviet Artists, 1965.

BOOKS ILLUSTRATED BY DEGAS

La Maison Tellier by Guy de Maupassant. Paris: Ambroise Vollard, 1934.

Mimes et courtisanes by Pierre Louys. Paris: Ambroise Vollard, 1934.

Degas, Danse et Dessin by Paul Valéry. Paris: Ambroise Vollard, 1936, 1950.

La Famille Cardinal by L. Halévy. Paris: A. Blairet & Fils, 1938.

CATALOGUES OF DEGAS EXHIBITIONS

Etchings by Degas. Preface and notes by P. Moss. University of Chicago, 1964.

Degas, his Family and Friends in New Orleans. Essays by J. Rewald, J.B. Byrnes and J.S. Boggs. Isaac Delgado Museum, New Orleans, 1965.

Drawings by Degas. Text by J.S. Boggs. Saint Louis City Art Museum; Philadelphia Museum of Art; Minneapolis Society of Fine Arts, 1967.

Lithographs by Degas. Preface by W.M. Ittman Jr. Washington University, Saint Louis, Missouri and University Museum, Lawrence, Kansas, 1967.

Degas Monotypes. Text by E.P. Janis. Fogg Art Museum, Cambridge, Mass., 1968.

Degas Racing World. Wildenstein Galleries, New York, 1968.

Degas. Œuvres du Musée du Louvre. Text by H. Adhémar. Orangerie, Paris, 1969.

Degas. Pastels and Drawings. University Art Gallery, Nottingham, England, 1969.

Edgar Degas. 1834-1917. Text by D. Sutton. Lefevre Gallery, London, 1970.

Edgar Degas. The Reluctant Impressionist. Preface by B.S. Shapiro. Museum of Fine Arts, Boston, 1974.

Degas Bronzes. Museum of Fine Arts, Dallas, 1974.

Works by Degas in the Detroit Institute of Arts. Text by T. Reff. Detroit, 1974-75.

Degas. Preface by J. Cau. Galerie Schmit, Paris, 1975.

The Complete Sculptures of Degas. Preface by J. Rewald. Lefevre Gallery, London, 1976.

Degas in the Metropolitan. Text by T. Reff. Metropolitan Museum of Art, New York, 1977.

Edgar Degas. Text by T. Reff. Acquavella Galleries, New York, 1978.

Degas. 1879. Catalogue by R. Pickwance. National Gallery of Scotland, Edinbourg, 1979.

Degas and the Dance. Catalogue by L.M. Muehlig. Smith College Museum of Art, Northampton, Mass., 1979.

Degas. La famille Bellelli. Variations autour d'un chef-d'œuvre. Musée Marmottan, Paris, 1980.

Mary Cassatt and Edgar Degas. Text by N.M. Mathews. San José Museum of Art, Cal., 1981.

The Sculpture of Degas. Royal Museum and Public Library, Canterbury, England, 1982.

Degas. Kunsthalle, Tübingen; Nationalgalerie, Berlin, 1984.

Degas Sculptors. Centro Mostre di Firenze, Palazzo Strozzi, 1986.

The Private Degas. Catalogue by Richard Thompson. Whitworth Art Gallery, Manchester. Fitzwilliam Museum, Cambridge.

ILLUSTRATIONS